C++ and Data Analytics 2 Bundle Manuscript

Essential Beginners Guide on Enriching Your C++ Programming Skills and Learn Practical Data Analytics, Data Science, and Predictive Analytics for Beginners

Series: Hacking Freedom and Data Driven (C++ & Data Analytics)

By Isaac D. Cody

C++ AND
DATA ANALYTICS

2 BUNDLE MANUSCRIPT

Essential Beginners Guide on Enriching Your C++
Programming Skills and Learn Practical Data Analytics, Data
Science, and Predictive Analytics for Beginners

ISAAC D. CODY

QUICK TABLE OF CONTENTS

This book will contain 2 manuscripts from the Hacking Freedom and Data Driven series. It will essentially be two books into one.

The first part of this book will dive into learning the sophisticated programming language of C++ and get you on your way to program like a boss!

Data Analytics will start your journey and learn the fundamentals of Data Analytics and how you can apply it to your business.

C++: Learn C++ Like a Boss

A Beginners Guide in Coding Programming And Dominating C++. Novice to Expert Guide To Learn and Master C++ Fast

By: Isaac D. Cody

C++

LEARN C++ LIKE A BOSS

A BEGINNERS GUIDE IN CODING PROGRAMMING AND DOMINATING C++

Novice to expert guide to learn
and master C++ FAST

ISAAC D. CODY

within this book are for clarifying purposes only and are the owned by the owners themselves, not affiliated with this document.

Table of Contents

Chapter 1: Basic Background, History, and the Fruition of C++

Before we get into how to start using C++, you have to learn what it is, and how it came about. The reason for this is simple. To truly know something, you have to know everything you possibly can learn about the subject, especially when it comes to something so technical such as computer programming.

C++ is a very important part of computer and Internet history. It is simply something that is interwoven within the history of the technological world, as we know today. Furthermore, the apps and other functions on a smart phone would not exist if it were not for C++.

When you are learning C++, you will be filled with wonder at the fact that one programming language can have so much impact in our daily lives. Almost every computer ever built can be attributed to a specific aspect that can be traced back to the language of C++. One of the benefits of learning this language is the ability to learn other languages with ease. Having the ability of learning C++ will enhance your knowledge of other programming language, which is why many people regard it as the 'godfather' of computer programming. Furthermore, many big companies still need programmers that have C++ as they rely this programming language to run their central computer system. So when the going gets tough, just know it'll benefit you in the long run so stay strong and get in the programming mindset!

History of C++

Bjarne Strousup was working on his thesis for his doctorate, and he decided to work with a programming language that was known as Simula. This language one one of the first programming languages of the computer age. However it was very slow and full of bugs.

Strousup came up with the idea of C with Classes. A programming language that was a lot faster than Simula. C with classes later became Cfront which sped up the process of creating a language. However, Cfront was left in the dust when C++ came along, because it added compilers into the language, making it a lot easier, and faster to use than any other project language of the time.

Since then there have been annotated reference guides and updates to the language to make it better and faster, and even easier to use. C++ for Dummies is a popular guide for this language.

C++ is one of the most popular languages out there today. This language is the best for many industries, so rather than make a new language which takes a lot of time, they just adapt C++ to many different variations because it is versatile in its nature.

Exactly what is C++

C++ is not just any programming language, it is object oriented. Object oriented programming or OOP for short, is programming that revolves around objects rather than actions. It is like looking at the whole picture at once, rather than each individual puzzle piece.

This programming language was designed with flexibility and speed in mind, as other languages of the time were way too slow, and could only do one thing, so every time you wanted to create something new, you needed a new language.

There are many things that you can use this language for, and they are still very much popular today, despite the ominous amount of languages that are out there now.

- Prepackaged scripts: These are what script enthusiasts, and new hackers use to practice their programming techniques. Since so many people nowadays want to take the easy way out, scripts that come already prepared are what most hackers are looking for, thus the packages need to improve, and they do so using C++.

- Video Games: Let's face it, pretty much everyone plays video games at some point in their life. Whether it is growing up, or when you have kids, you will get sucked into the realm of video games, and you can never escape. Those games can be attributed to some way or form from using the C++ language. If you are into making games, and bringing the world joy through graphics, then it is definitely a good idea to learn the language of C++

- Web pages: A lot of web pages are made using C++. The reason for this is because the language is so easy to manipulate, it makes for a quick and easy website that has plenty of interactive features for people. Some websites you may visit often that are created with C++ are Amazon and Ebay. If you like designing web pages you should learn C++ to be efficient and maybe even land a decent job in this field.

- Phone Apps: Nowadays it seems everyone has a smart phone, and that means apps galore. There are thousands of apps out there, and more are being made every day. Some apps are free, some apps cost money, but a good chunk were made using C++. That is because this language is so scalable that it can be used for simple games and more intricate shopping apps.

There are a lot of other minor things that C++ is used for, such as VoIP calling. That was created using C++. The fact of the matter is, you will get told time and time again that C++ is a dying language when in reality that is just a ruse that JAVA people uses to scare people into switching languages to ensure that C++ is a dying language.

Why It's used

C++ is used not only for its flexibility and speed, but because it has a lot of components, it is fairly easy to learn, and if you master C++, you can master the other languages with ease. The reason for this is that when you learn something that is a little more complex than everything else first, the easier stuff will fall right into place, however, if you get used to easy to learn subjects, then you will find that the more difficult stuff is hard to learn because you are not used to putting in that much effort into the subject that you are trying to learn.

If you want to learn a language that you can use for different types of functions within the realm of computer technology, then this is the language for you. You can do almost anything with it, and once you learn enough about it, you may be able to figure out ways to manipulate the language to do things that it generally cannot do.

C++ is a very important language when it comes to computer programming, and though it has a lot of variables from the way that it is laid out, it is very easy to read, and very easy to create. This makes it one of the most desired programming languages that are out there, because no one wants to struggle to read code. No one wants to have to spend all of their time out there working on what they know is right just because they cannot find where they went wrong.

Job Outlook

Yes, there are a lot of jobs out there that still rely on C++ to operate. There are so many different things that you could do, and all of them affect other people in the community. Video game designing, and web page designing are two of the most prominent things that are out there. You could also become a white hat or blue hat hacker.

But according to payscale.com (search software engineer), a person with C++ Software engineer background can earn up to $57,000 to $120,000 based on experience. The median is around $80,363. Some other titles that people with C++ programming language have is Computer Programmer, Electrical Engineer, and Application Developer.

However, to be the best that you can be, you should always know two or three programming languages to be marketable. Though those languages will not be included in this book, do not marry yourself to a single language. Instead, just like with human language, broaden your horizons and dabble in a few, but keep one as your main language.

C++ should be the main language that you fall back on due to its versatility. Maybe use JAVA or Linux as your other languages, but C++ is the best main language to have, and you only want the best as your main.

C++ is a statically written lower level language which means that it is a clean cut expansive language.

C++ is a fully functional super set of C that supports object oriented programming. This means that it supports all the pillars of OOP, such as encapsulation, data hiding, inheritance and polymorphism.

To learn more about object oriented programming, you can do a quick search online, and find out more about it. It is best to get some knowledge about what it is, but it is not quintessential to your knowledge of C++, so it will not really be included in this book, except for a few mentions in passing, and some tidbits of information here and there.

Three Important Components of C++

The standard C++ is made up of three very important concepts.

- Core Language: This is made up of all the variables, data types, literals, and other important aspects of the language, creating building blocks to get to the next level

- C++ Standard Library: this allows you to manipulate files, and other workings within the language, and bend them to your will.

- STL: This stands for Standard Template Library, which gives you functions to manipulate data structures and variables and other things of the sort.

Why is C++ considered the best language out there?

Well, aside from the copiously mentioned flexibility, speed, and simplicity, it is a language that has spanned over thirty years, and is still widely used today. There are not many products in any genre of life out there that can say the same. Products and companies come and go, but only true perfection stays. Well that is how the saying goes. To be honest, C++ has had many updates since then, but the core process is still the same. When it came out it was light years ahead of its time, and today it is still a pretty advanced piece of technology, due to the updates that keep it on top.

There are a lot of opinions that also have to do with why C++ is considered the best. While there are a lot of people who say that C++ is no longer relevant, even more vouch that it is still the best language out there, and it is their fall back language. It is the one they know the most about, and the one they carry close to their heart. The reasons vary, but the fact that 90% of programmers default to C++ shows that it is very much the best programming language out there today.

C++ is one of the few languages that follow the ANSI standard completely, which is why some of the best games you will ever play are still written with C++. Because their compilers are set to ensure that all commands are written and executed without errors. It can also be used across many different types of platforms, whether you have a Microsoft, Unix, Mac, Windows, or and Alpha device, it is possible to use C++. This is a great thing, because a lot of programmers have to operate across many different platforms, and the universality makes it easy and portable. Just throw your code on a flash drive and upload it wherever it is needed.

Benefits of using the C++ language

There are a lot of benefits that you will be able to enjoy when using the C++ language. Some of these benefits include:

- The big library: since C++ has been around for along time, they have a library that is pretty large. This is available for you to use so you can pick out the codes that you want inside of your script and save some time and even learn some new things. You can also create some of your own codes if you wish, but this library can be really helpful for the beginner who is learning and can make it easier than ever to get the code written.

- Ability to work with other languages: C++ is a great language to use with some of the other programming languages out there. This makes it easier to really work on the projects that you want because you can add in the parts that you like from different coding languages and combine them together to get something really amazing.

- Works on many projects: most other programming languages are going to focus on just one or two little projects. For example, using JavaScript means that you are just going to be working on websites. But with C++, you are able to use it to help with a lot of different projects. Whether you are looking to work on a website, looking to create a new program, or do something else with programming, you will be able to do it with the help of C++.

- Fast and reliable: if you have used some of the other coding languages that are popular in the past, you will find that sometimes they aren't the most reliable. Information may slip through or they won't start working the way that you would like. If you want something that works the first time and is reliable, then it is a good idea to go with C++.

- Offers a lot of power: those who like to work in programming and want to have a lot of power in the work that they are doing will find that C++ is the right option for them to choose. It has some of the best power for the programming languages that are out there.

These are just a few of the benefit that you can enjoy when you are using the C++ programming language. It may seem a bit more difficult to use than some of the others, such as Python, but it has a lot of the power that you need and can work well with other programming languages. With a bit of practice, you are going to get all the basics of this language down and really enjoy what you are able to do with this programming language.

Chapter 2: Let's Begin

Let's begin! There are a lot of places we can start, but let's talk about environments first. While you do not really need to set up your own environment, as there are many online. An environment is a compiler of your choice that takes your code, and does all of the functions for you. In the old days, you would have to open your command prompts and create an environment to use, but those days are over. A simple mistake back in the day could do some serious damage to their computers. Now you can practice some risky prompts without any risk to your device whatsoever.

There are many examples to try out and use on the internet. To try them out, the easiest place to go is http://www.compileonline.com Choose the "Learn C++" option down at the bottom, and it will take you to where you need to go.

Here is an example to try. The output should be the words "**Try This**".

```
#include <iostream>

using namespace std;

int main ()
{
        court << "Use This One!";

        return 0;
}
```

Now you can choose to type these codes into the compiler directly, or you can write several, and save them to your computer, and access them whenever, so that you don't have to retype them every time you want to mess with them. You can use several different types of text editors. However, some of them are device type specific. This means they only work on the type of device that you create them on.

The text editors that you can use are OS edit command, Brief, EMACS, epsilon, Windows Notepad, vlm or vl. However, only vlm and vl are multi platform usable. Make sure to save the files with the extension .c or .cpp.

You should start in a text editor to get the rough draft going on your program before you even think of moving to a compiler. This is because once you get to a compiler, it is a lot easier to mess up on your program, and not catch it. However, if you have it laid out in a nice, clean-cut fashion in a text editor, then you should have no problems with getting things going in the compiler.

C++ Compilers

There are many different compilers out there, and a lot of them are pretty expensive. Those compilers are for the elite programmers who have mastered the lower level compilers already. Beginners only need a basic compiler, and most of those are free. However, just like with anything that is free, you have to be careful of what you are getting. There are more bad cheap compliers than good ones out there so on the pretense of being free, I would suggest you paying additional functions past the start up page. These additional functions are usually very cheap anyways so you won't have to break the bank to get them.

One of the most popular compilers available is the GNU C/C++ compiler. It is used most commonly in UNIX and Linux installations. To see if you already have the compiler, pull up the command line in your UNIX/Linux application and type in the following

```
$ g++ -v
```

If the compiler is installed, then you should see this message on the screen:

Using built-in specs.

Target: i386-redhat-linux

Configured with: ../configure –prefix=/usr ......

Thread model: posix

gcc version 4.1.2 20080704 (Red Hat 4.1.2-46)

If this message does not come up on your screen, the compiler either isn't on the computer or you installed it incorrectly and you will need to go through and get it properly installed.

In this book, we will go over how to install using the Windows platform. If you have a different platform, then you should go to http://gcc.gnu.org/install/ and read the instructions on how to download it onto your platform.

To install this compiler on your Windows computer, you will need to first install MinGW. This is the software that makes the compiler compatible with your computer, and it is very important that you have this software, otherwise you will not even be able to download the compiler at all.

To install this software, you can go to the homepage of the software at www.mingw.org and allow it to direct you to where you need to go. Once you install that you should install gcc core, gcc-g++, MinGW runtime and blnutlls, at the bare minimum, but you can install more if you would like. Once you are done with the install, you can run all of the GNU tools from the Command line on Windows.

Now that you have everything set up to where you can run it, you can start learning more about how to run the programs themselves.

Basic Syntax

C++ can be defined as not only the program, but objects that collectively communicate by invoking other methods. When you are working with C++ you should know what four things mean above all else.

Class- This is a template or a blueprint that states the object and its support type, and describes the behaviors of an object. This means that objects are sorted by their behaviors and their actions /supports into classes that fit the description of the object in question.

Object- Objects have behaviors and states. For example, if you look at a dog, it has states. These states could be classified as color, breed, name, standard of breed (AKC/AKA/APC registries). "Dogs" also show certain behaviors as well. They wag their tails, they bark, they pant, they eat dry kibble, and they go to the bathroom outside in the yard. These things make dogs a *unique object*. These objects are classified into groups know as, you guessed it, classes.

Method- This is another term for behavior. There can be as many or as few as you choose in your classes. This is where all of the data is manipulated, and actions are played out, along with the place that all of the logic is written. Methods are especially important because without them, your program would not know what it is supposed to do with the variable that you give it. It would just sit there like a dud and do nothing.

Instant Variables- These refer to each individual object. Each object is classified with a unique set of these variables that act as a fingerprint for an object. These variables are assigned to the object by using values that occur whenever the object is created.

Now that you know the four main definitions of programming, Let's take a look at a code that you can write that will print out: **"Try This"**. Unlike the example above, this will explain a little more in depth what you are wanting to do, and the reason for each function.

```
#include <iostream>

using namespace std;


// main() [this is when the program will begin to execute.]


int main()
{
```

```
        cout << "Try This"; // [Prints Try This]

        return 0;

}
```

This function will allow you to print whatever you want, not just the words "Try This".

Now let's break down the various aspects of the program that is set out above. There are several different aspects of this language that you have to take in consideration. Each aspect is important in getting it to run, and if you do not execute them entirely.

Headers- There are several headers out there for C++, and all of them are necessary or at the very least useful to your programming operations. However, for most functions you will see the header that is above <iostream>. When you use a header be sure to enclose it properly, and put **#include before** it to prompt the program to use that header.

Namespace- Namespaces are a fairly new addition to C++, only coming about in the 2011 update. They do not do much, other than describe which namespace to use. While they are not necessary, they save you a lot of confusion on functions of a program. It simply act as a way to organize your functions more systematically.

Main- Here is where the main function begins. Using the line **// main()** instructs the program to start executing the main function of the program, and start the out put process. It is essential that you set up the main function command, otherwise your program will not know what it is supposed to be running, nor will it know when it is supposed to run. This will be seen as a single line comment inside the program and it is going to tell the program that the main function is beginning.

INT main- This is where the function execution officially begins. If you do not include this, the entire process will stop, because you did not introduce the variables, and without the variables, the program is lost.

Cout- This instructs the program to display the message that you want on the screen. If you do not put cout, chances are your program will may or may not fail. The problem is you don't know if you succeed or not so if you want to make sure that everything runs smoothly, be sure to add cout.

Return- This returns the value back to zero, and terminates the function. It instructs the program to end the process, and go back to the beginning.

Now to compile and execute your first official C++ program.

First you must know how to *save* the file. Open your chosen text editor, and enter the code that is seen above. Once you have done that, hit save as, and choose a file location that is easily found. For organization purposes, it is always best to have a separate folder for all of your programs. Save the file as hello.cpp, and once you have saved it, you should open up your command prompt before heading to the directory where the file is saved.

To get the file to open inside your compiler, start by typing 'g++ hello.cpp'. you can then press enter and the code will be opened properly. As long as there aren't any errors, the prompt is going to generate an a.out executable file. To run the program, type out 'o.out' and see the compiler work. The information that you should get on the compiler from this on the computer includes:

```
$ g++ hello.cpp

$ ./a.out
```

Try This

Make sure that you are inputting all of the variables the proper way, and remember, these things are case sensitive. If you do not input the functions the right way, you will find that things tend to go awry. The thing with coding is you have to be precise. This detailed oriented personal attributed applies to all programming languages! However, anyone can do it if they are willing to pay attention.

The basic function commands are not the only things that you need to use. There are other things that are important when you are building a prompt as well, as they too instruct the program to do specific things. Some of these things are blocks and semicolons.

You probably think a pause in a sentence when you think semicolon, however, they are complete stops in C++ programs. The semicolon indicates the termination of a statement. This means that each individual statement must be indicated by the use of a semicolon. The following are three different statements.

x=y;

y=y+1;

add(x,y);

Each one of those statements were separated by not only a line break, but also a semicolon. You could also do it this way.

x=y; y=y+1; add(x,y);

Each one of those will be recognized as separate statements simply because of the semicolon. It is kind of mind blowing how something so simple can have so much of an impact.

In this coding language, a block is going to be a set of statements that you enclose with brackets. These statements are logical entities that the program puts on the screen due to the main command prompt. For example

```
{
        cout << "I like Pizza">>; //prints I like
Pizza

        return 0
}
```

The end of a line is not a terminator, as was indicated above. The semicolon is the only thing that terminates the statement.

Identifiers

Now let us move on to the identifiers in the program. These identifiers are used to identify multiple things, such as classes, modules, functions and variables within a block. An identifier is going to be a group of letters and numbers that you are able to name your program or your files and they must start with a letter, but can have any letter or number you want afterwards. There are no punctuation characters other than what you might see in a sentence that are allowed as identifiers. You will not see characters such as @,&,% or $, and the programming is case sensitive. That means YokoOno is different than Yokoono, yokoOno, and yokoono. Make sure that you are capitalizing only the letters that you should be capitalizing in your programs.

Though pretty much anything can be an identifier, there are some things that are reserved for keywords in C++, and can't be used as identifiers. These words are as follows.

asm		
Break	Bool	Auto
Char	Catch	Case
Const cast	Const	Class
Delete	Default	Continue
Dynamic cast	Double	Do
Explicit	Enum	Else
False	Extern	Export
Friend	For	Float
Inline	If	Goto
Mutable	Long	Int
Protected	Private	Namespace
Reinterpret cast	Register	Public
Signed	Short	Return
Static cast	Static	Sizeof
Template	Switch	Struct
True	Throw	This
Typeid	Typedef	Try
Unsigned	Unlon	Typename

Void	Virtual	Using
While	Wchar t	Volatile

Everything else is fair game when it comes to identifiers. Think of identifiers as usernames and passwords. Mix it up, but make sure that they are functional.

Trigraphs

Trigraphs are going to be sequences of three characters that will represent just one character. You will notice these because they are going to start out with two questions marks at the beginning. Seems a little redundant to use three characters when one will work, but the reason behind this is so you do not confuse the program with the meaning of the character, as many are similar.

Here are some frequently used trigraphs to give you an example of what we mean.

??=	#
??/	\
??'	^
??(	[
??)	]
??!	|
??<	{
??>	}
??-	~

Not all compilers support trigraphs due to their confusing nature, and most people try to stay away from them, however, it has been found that when you memorize trigraphs, you are less likely to mess up by hitting the wrong symbol in your function.

Whitespace

Moving on to whitespace. This is the empty lines in a program. Sometimes they contain comments, and these are known as blank lines. The compilers completely ignore them. Whitespace describes blanks, new lines, tabs, characters and comments. It is merely used to make your program look more organized and readable.

There should be at least one line of whitespace between the variable/identifier and the statement.

QUIZ

You thought that you could just waltz through this book without being tested on if you were paying attention? No cheating either! Just because you can peek at the answers does not mean that you should. You should take it just like a normal quiz to truly test your knowledge so you can figure out if you need to go back and re-read over some things. This is a short quiz, so you will be okay.

1.   What is whitespace?

2.   Fill in the blanks ____ <<x=y+1_>>

3.   What are trigraphs?

4.   Who Invented the C with Classes language?

5.   What is the header used in most functions?

Answers

1.   The blank spaces or comments that the compiler ignores

2.   Cout <<x=y+1;>>

3.   A sequence of three characters that represent a single character

4.   Bjarne Strousup

5.   <iostream>

Congratulations, if you got all five right, then you can move on to the next section! However, if you got more than one wrong, then you should probably go back and reread the section. If you're ready then onwards to Chapter 3.

Chapter 3: Diving more into Program Comments, Data Types, Lines, and Characters

Now that we have covered the bare basics of C++ it is time to get into some more in depth subjects that surround the program. While these are more in depth, they are still a paramount concepts all beginners need to learn.

Program Comments

So, there are going to be times when you will want to write some comments inside of your code. These are important because they allow you to leave a little message inside the code so that others who are reading through it later on will be able to get a good look at exactly how your code is ran and also provide "referral" to what you're trying to accomplish in your code. Furthermore, leaving notes within the lines of your code is a good way to notify yourself where a code might have gone wrong. By putting comments inside your codes, you are more likely to know where you succeed or where you went wrong.

These comments can be as simple or as complex as you would like. Some people will just place in one or two words if that is all that is needed to help out the other users, but there are other times when you are going to need to combine a few more lines into the mix to ensure that it is all going to work out and that the other person understands what is going on inside of the code.

In this language, you will just need to use the // symbol in order to show that you are writing out a comment. You can make it as long as you would like, just make sure that when the comment is done, you skip to the next line so that the program knows that it is supposed to start reading through it again.

The program is going to stop reading after the // and it is not going to affect the way that the program works. Other programmers who look at the code will see the comments that you write, but when the program is executed, these comments are going to be skipped. You can add in as many as you would like to your program, but do try to keep them a bit limited because it can start to clog up the code and make it hard to read and understand.

Program comments are basically the statements that are inside the code. The statements, or comments, are going to be there to help others who use your code understand what the purpose of each function is. All program languages allow for some type of comments, but they do not allow all of the kinds of comments that are out there. The most common to use is a single line comment. This is what all program languages allow for. These comments are simple explanatory lines that tell the next reader what the purpose is in a simple sentence.

There are also multiple line comments. This is one that very few program languages allow for. C++ is one of those few languages. Sometimes you have a more complex explanation, and it needs to span over more than one line. This is possible to do in C++.

When you are using a single line comment, you will see that it is written out in the code with //
and can go all the way to the end of your line. An example of this is:

```
{
        cout << "that's great" >>;  //prints that's great

        return 0
}
```

will have the final output of "that's great" and nothing else. The comment is ignored by the compiler so that you can let other programmers in on what the code is for, or what you need done to the code.

However if you are trying to get some help on a code, you should use a multi line comment so that you can easily get the best out of your complicated code. Multi line comments are surrounded by these symbols /*-*/. Typed out like that it almost looks like an emoji. For example

/* I need help making the puppet dance*/ is a comment. However, that is still a single line comment still. A better example would be

/* I need help making the puppet dance

*All he does at this point is sway from side to side */

That would be a multi line comment. As you can see, when you start a new line you should put the asterisk at the beginning to indicate to the program that you are still writing a comment and that the next line is indeed whitespace. When compiled it will ignore the comments and only show what you want it to show.

While you can mix the comment styles, it is best to keep them separated for now, until you get the hang of everything.

Data Types

You have to use different variables when you are writing a program using any language. These are nothing more than just reserved memory values that store locations in some space in the memory of the compiler. The above list of reserved keywords are useful here as well. While there are a lot of keywords, there are seven basic keywords that define data types.

Type	Keyword
Wide character	Wchar_t
Valueless	Void
Double floating point	Double
Floating point	Float
Integer	Int
Character	Char
Boolean	bool

Most of the data types that you can use can be modified using one of these following modifiers to help:

Long,

Short

Unsigned

Signed

Variable Types Cont...

When you are using variables inside of a coding language, you are providing some storage space that makes it easier to for the program to manipulate. All of the variables that you use will be attached to a different type and these types are going to determine the layout and the size of the memory of the variable. It is also going to set a range of values that you are able to store on this memory space.

Naming the variable is going to be similar to naming the identifier. You will only be able to name it with a letter or an underscore and the letters are going to be case sensitive. But after that, you are able to use any type of digit, letter, and character that you would like.

Again, the basic variables that you will be able to use here in more detail include:

• Wchart_t: this is the wide character type.

• Void: this is going to represent the absence of a type

• Double: this is a floating value that will have double precision.

• Float: this is a floating point that is going to have single precision.

• Int: this is an integer

• Char: this is often going to be just one byte and is a type of integer.

• Bool: this is going to work with values that are either true or false.

You can also define other types of variables. These variables are things line pointer, array, reference, enumeration, data structures, and classes.

Creating a new line

Now that you know the data types and modifiers, and all about making a comment in your program, it is time to learn about how to create a new line. This is a problem that a lot of new programmers run into. They have their program all nice and laid out in the input, but the output is still really mashed together and really unkempt. This is because they did not properly create a new line. Remember that whitespace is ignored, so you cannot just skip a line, and expect to have a line skipped in your program. You have to indicate to the compiler that you want to start a new line. This is really important, as when you play out your program, you want it to run smoothly. You do not want to see something like this.

Try This Today I ate Pizza and I did math. 6= (7-1) that what I learned today.

You would probably rather see this.

Try This

today I ate pizza and I did math

6=(7-1)

that is what I learned today

To make the distinction, you have to have the right function, as that is what programming relies on, having the correct function.

To create a line break, you have to use the function endl; this will indicate that you want a line break, and you do not even have to add whitespace if you do not want to, though it is recommended because it makes your program easier to read for a human.

For example, this:

```
{
        cout << Try This;>> endl;

        <<Today I ate Pizza and did Math;>>
endl;

        <<6=(7-1);>> endl;

        << That is what I learned today;>> endl;

        return 0

}
```

Looks way better than this:

```
{
        cout << Try This;>> endl; << Today I
ate Pizza and did Math;>> endl; <<6=(7-1);>>
endl; << That is what I learned today;>> endl;

        return 0

}
```

Can you see how confusing that would get for someone reading the code? You want your code file to be easy to read, so that if someone else has to fix something, they can easily find where the mistake has been made. If everything is all jumbled together, then they would not be able to find anything very easily, now would they?

You can also indicate line breaks by using /n This is the same thing as endl; but is a lot faster to type. You can use whichever method you want but choose one and stick with it.

The importance of the basics of C++

I know what you are thinking, why must you know all these nonsense tidbits of information when you are just beginning, and the reason is, if you don't learn them now, you won't think that you will need them in the future, and then when you are reading a program that someone else wrote, you will be wondering what all of those extra characters mean, and why there is so much whitespace. Creating a habit of these simple yet somewhat tedious tasks is paramount if mastering more complicated programming methods. Just like mastering any sort of language, you have to master the basics to master the expert level concepts.

Variable definitions

A variable definitions instructs the compiler how much and where to store and create the variable. It specifies the data type and lists one or more of the variables of the type. For example

type variable_list;

You have to have a valid data type that is listed above. They may contain one or more identifier names as long as they are separated by commas, such as

int ---- j,k,l;

char----c,ch;

float---- f, salary;

double--- d;

Each of these abbreviations instructs the compiler to create variables of that type with those names. Variables can be assigned with an initial value, by indicating such with an equal sign. For example

```
#include <iostream>

using namespace std;

int. main ()
int j=10;
int k=5;
int l=j+k
{
        cout <<l>> endl;

        return 0
}
```

You should get the answer 15

You can also declare and define the variables in your program, but that is some higher level stuff, so if you would like to look into it you can google search a tutorial on that.

QUIZ

Here is the set up. You should have one phrase, a math problem, and then the answer to the math problem using said integers. You can make up all of the variables yourself, whatever you want them to be.

```
#using <header>

using namespace std;


int main ()

int _=_
```

```
int _=_

int _=_+_

{

        cout < "";> /n

        < "";> /n

        cout  < "int_";> /n

        return 0

}
```

Simply enter your digits in and make sure your numbers add up. After you've done so, rerun the code without relying on copying and pasting the code without the intergers. This way, you'll have a basic understanding of variables and playing with the basic integers operations within C++.

Chapter 4: Arrays, Loops, and Conditions

Believe it or not, you've learned so much already. The basics are really not that hard and now it's just about learning about a few more things and putting concept after concept together to make sure you're becoming a better C++ programmer. Let's keep going.

Arrays

Arrays are a data structure in C++ that will be able to store elements that are basically the same type and also a fixed size. Basically a collection of same type variables. Instead of using the individual variables, you would declare one array of variables such as numbers. To do this you use the numbers 0 to 99 and access each one by an index of the array.

Arrays are going to be memory locations that are continuous. The lowest is always the first element and then the highest element is going to be the last.

Initializing arrays

You can initialize arrays one by one or using a single statement. Example

double balance [5]= {1000.0, 2.0, 3.4, 17.0, 50.0};

The numbers that are found between the bracket can't end up higher than the amount of elements that you are using. This means that you cannot have six sets of numbers when your array title only specified five. However, if you do not specify the size, then an array of just the right size is created. You would type it as follows double balance [] {1000.0, 2.0, 3.4, 17.0, 50.0};

This creates the exact same array as the previous example, only you did not specify the array size so it was created for you. Pretty nifty.

Now that you know how to write an array, it is time to move on to putting it into the actual program. This program is a bit more advanced than the ones before, and has a few more elements. You can look up these elements on www.compileonline.com. You will be directed to a lot of tutorials and there is even a PDF file for you to download.

Here is the formula for your program to assign an array.

#include <iostream>

```cpp
using namespace std;

#include <iomanip>
using std::setw;

int main ()
{
        int n[ 10 ];  //n is an array of ten
integers
        // initialize elements of array n to 0
        for ( int i=0; I <10; i++)
        {
                n[i] =i+100; // set ekement at
location I to i+ 100
        }
        cout << element << setw(13) <<
value<< endl:
        //output each array element's value
        for (int j=0; j<10; j++)
        {
                cout << setw(7)<< j << setw(13)
<<n[j] << endl;
        }
```

```
    return 0

}
```

This program was able to use the setw() function in order to format the output that you see.

Loop Types

The loop types are used any time that you would like to take one type of code and execute it over and over. These statements are going to be done one right after the other. The loop statement will make it easier to execute these statements as many times as you would like.

There are four types of loops. These loops handle different requirements.

While loop

The While loop is going to continue repeating the loop as long as a certain condition is met. It is going to test out this condition each time it restarts the loop cycle and will do this until the condition is no longer true.

Written like this

```
while (condition)
{
        statement(s);
}
```

For Loop

This loop executes a statement sequence over and over again while abbreviating the code that manages the loop variables.

Written like this

```
for ( init; condition; increment)
{
        statement(s);
}
```

Do.. while loop

The Do...while loop is going to be similar to the while statement, but it is going to test the condition when you reach the end of your statement, rather than the beginning.

Written like this

```
do
    {
            statement(s);
}while (condition);
```

Nested loops

The nested loop is going to have a loop that works inside of another loop, to create a continuous loop of loops. This one can get confusing after awhile.

Written like this

```
while (condition)
{
        while (condition)
        {
                statement(s)
```

```
        }

        statement(s) // you can put more
statements

}
```

Why is this important

Eventually you are going to want to branch out.
I would highly recommend to further enhance
your C++knowledge of the basics to ensure
mastery and better understanding of more
difficult tasks.

Though these may seem like they are too
advanced for some or too easy for others, it's
always good to do other practices and tutorials
to enrich your programming skills. You can
find tutorials at www.compileonline.com. It
cannot be stressed enough how much of an
essential tool this is. You have to check it out
for yourself, and find out just how useful it
really is. There are tutorials for other languages
as well, not just C++ dabble around and see
what you like.

Chapter 5: Working with Operators in C++

With any of the coding languages that you plan to use, it is important that you learn how to use the operators. These are going to help you to tell the program what you would like to do and can make dealing with your own codes so much easier. There are four main types of operators that you are able to use inside your program and they will each tell the program how to behave in a different way. Some of the operators that you will be able to use with the C++ language include:

- Logical operators

- Arithmetic operators

- Assignment operators

- Relational operators

Let's take a look at how some of these work and how you can bring them out to work well when writing code in the C++ language.

Logical operators

The first type of operator that we are going to use in this guidebook are the logical operators. These are going to help you to compare some of the parts that you are putting into the system. Some of the logical operators that you can work with include:

• (||): this is known as the logical OR. With this one, the condition is going to be true if one of your operands is not zero.

• (&&): this one is known as the logical AND. If you have two operands and they are not zero, your condition is true.

• (!): this is the logical NOT. You will be able to use this to reverse the status of your operand. So if the condition ends up being false, this sign will make it true.

Arithmetic operators

Another of the operators that you are able to use is the arithmetic operators. These are pretty much the same as using math in school. You are going to tell the program to add, subtract, and do other equations with the information that you are providing. Some of the arithmetic operators that you are able to use include:

- (+): this is the addition operator that will add together two operands of your choices.

- (-): this is the subtraction operator. It is going to take the right hand operand and subtract it from the left hand operand.

- (*): this is the operator that makes it possible to do multiplication in the C++ language.

- (/): this operator helps you to do division in C++.

- (++): this is the increment operator. It is going to increase the value of your operand by one.

• (--): this is the decrement operator. It is going to decrease the operand value by just one.

Assignment operators

The assignment operators will make it easier for you to assign a name to your variable and can help with searching for, saving, and so on with the different parts of the code that you are writing. Some of the assignment operators that you may use inside of C++ include:

• (=): this operator is the simple assignment operator. It is going to assign the value of the operand on the right hand to the one that is on the left.

• (+): this one is called the Add AND operator. It is going to add together the values from both operands and then assigns the sum of these over to the operand on the left side.

• (*=): this is the Multiply AND operator. It is going to multiply both of the operands and then gives the results over to the operand on the left side.

• (-=): this is the one that will subtract the value of your operand on the right side from the one on the left and then gives this difference to the left operand.

• (/=): this is the divide and operator. It is going to divide the value that is on the left side from the one on the right side and then assigns this amount to the left side.

There are a few other assignment operators that are available, but they are more advanced so we will just stick with some of these basic ones to help keep things in order!

Relational Operators

Relational operators can be really helpful when you are working inside of the C++ language. Some of the ones that you can use include:

• (==): this is the operator that is going to check the equality of your two operands. If they are equal, the conditions will be true.

• (>): this operator is going to check the value of your operands. If the operand on the left side is higher than the one on the right, the condition will be true.

• (<): this operator is basically the opposite of the one above. If you find that the value of your operand on the left side is greater than the one on the right side, the condition will be true.

• (!=): this one is going to check the equality of your two operands and if the values are unequal, your condition is true.

• (<=): this operator is going to check whether the operand on the left side is less than or equal to the operand on the right side. If it meets this criteria, the condition is true.

• (>=): this one is going to check if the value of the operand on the left side is greater or equal to the one on the right side. If it is true, the condition is true.

Chapter 6: Helping C++ to Make Decisions

There are times when you will need the program to make decisions for you. You are able to set it up to act in a certain way based on the information that the user puts into the computer and what you decide needs to be met for the conditions to be true. The decision making is a bit more advanced inside of this system, but you will find that is pretty easy to learn and will open up a lot of ideas that you are able to work with in the C++ system. Let's take a look at some of the things that you are able to do to help the system to make decisions on its own.

Switch Statements

The first decision that we are going to work with inside of this system are the switch statements. These statements are nice because they are going to allow you to check the equality of your variable against a set of values, or cases. The variable that you are trying to check is going to be compared with each of the cases. A good example of the syntax that you are able to use for this include:

```
Switch(expression){

        case constant-expression:

        statement(s);

        break; //optional

        case constant-expression:

        statement(s);

        break; //optional



//you can add in as many of these case
statements as you would like



Default: //Optional

statement(s);

}
```

When you are working inside of these statements, there are a few rules that you should keep in mind. First, the expression of the switch statement should be the integral or enumerated class type. In addition, it can also belong to a class that has a conversion function. With C++, there isn't going to be a limit to the amount of case statements that you add into the syntax so you can make them as long or short as you would like. Just remember that you need to have a colon and a value in each of them.

Once the variable finds a value that it is equal to, it is going to keep running until it finds a break statement. The system finds the break statement, the switch is going to stop. Then the control flow will be passed on. You don't need to put in a break statement to the cases. If you end up not having one of these, the control flow will just keep being passed on.

The if statements

One of the most basic things that you are able to do in your programs is create an if statement. These are going to be based on a true and false idea inside the system. If the system says that the input is true with the condition that you set out, then the program is going to run whatever you ask it to. For example, you set it up to have the system as what the answer to 2 + 2 is. If the user puts in the answer as 4, you could have a message come up that says "That is Correct! Good Job!"

Any time that the user puts in an input that ends up being true based on the conditions that you are setting out, you are going to get the statement to show up that you picked out. On the other hand, what is going to happen if your person puts in the wrong answer. If they put the answer as 5 to the question above, it is not going to be right and the system is going to see that the answer is false.

Since the if statement is pretty basic, you are going to find that it is not going to be prepared if the person puts in the wrong answer. At this stage, if they put in any number other than 4 for the example above, the screen is just going to go blank and nothing is going to happen. The next type of statement will go more in depth and show you how to get answers based on what the person puts into the system.

The if else statement

Now as we discussed a bit above, there are some limitations that can come up when you are using the if statement. If the person puts in the wrong answer, the screen is just going to go blank and this can be a pain with the system. Plus, there are times when the user will need to put in a variety of answers, such as when they will put in their age and you want to separate those out. Their age is not necessarily wrong, but if you just want people who are older than 21, you want to make sure that an answer comes up correctly along the way.

A good syntax to use in order to work with the if else statements include:

if(boolean_expresion)

{

        //statement(s) will execute if the boolean expression is true

}

Else

{

```
        // statement(s) will execute if the
boolean expression is false

}
```

You are able to add in as many of these into your statement as you would like. So if you would like to have a program that set apart people in five different age groups, you could set that up based on more of the "else" in your syntax. This makes it easier to add in some other choices.

So let's keep it simple. Let's say that you have 2 +2 on the system. If the person guesses that 4 is the answer, you can set that up in the first part to be the true statement and then the message "That's Right! Good Job!" will come up on the screen. But if the user puts in the answer 5 (or any other answer than 4), you can have a message like "Sorry, that is not the right answer" come up on the screen.

This gives you a lot of freedom when it comes to taking care of what you want to do inside of your code. You are going to be able to add in some different things to the process and you can really expand the code that you are working on.

Another thing that you can keep in mind when working on these, is that you are able to add some if statements and some if else statements inside of each other. This can get a bit complex as a beginner, but with some practice, you will find that it is going to add a lot of power to the whole process and can make it easier to do some of the things that you want within this coding language.

Working with the if statements and the if else statements can make your coding experience so much better. It allows the system to make decisions based on what the user is putting into the system rather than having to be there and do it themselves. Make sure to try out a few of these different types of statements and see how they are going to work within your code and with what you want to do.

Chapter 6: Constants and the various types of Literals

This language is complex, and even though what you have learned above is enough to run some simple functions, there are so many more parts to this language that it would be a crime to not put more in depth knowledge in here to help you transition to the next step.

If you want to be successful with this language, be prepared to spend long hours working hard on it. While it is a good language for beginners as it has multiple levels of difficulties, it is also something that you have to work hard at to make it to the next level. The added effects are more difficult the more you try to learn.

Programming itself is a long and difficult process, but it is definitely worth it, as there are so many professions that you can go into that require the knowledge of C++. From game designing, to working with robots and more. If it involves technology, chances are it involves C++.

So here are some more steps that you can learn, and some more important functions that you need to know to begin to master this language.

Constants and Literals

Constants and literals are an imperative part of learning C++. They refer to data types and variables in those data types. They are constant, and cannot be changed.

They act just like any other variable, other than the fact that they are stagnant and you cannot change them. The integers that you use are known as literal integers. They can have a suffix such as U or L, and they stand for unassigned, and long. These variables are used as uppercase and lowercase and can help your processes along well.

To understand the integer literals, look at some of these examples:

032uu	//illegal: can't repeat your suffix
078 octal digit	//illegal: 8 isn't considered an
Ox_Fell	//this one is legal
215	//this one is legal
212	//this one is legal
85	//this one is a decimal
30ul	//this one is an unsigned long
30l	//this one is long
30u	//this one is an unsigned int.
30	//tis one is an int.
Ox4b	//this one is a hexadecimal
0213	//this one is an octal

Floating Point Literals

These are parts of the code that will contain an integer, a decimal point, a fractional part, and an exponent part. These can be shown either through the exponential form or the decimal form.

When you choose to use the decimal point to represent these literals, you need to make sure that you are adding in at least the decimal, although adding in the exponent is good as well. When you are representing through the exponential form, you should include either the fractional part, the integer part, or both of them. The signed exponent that you are using should also be started with either E or e.

Some of the floating point literals that you are able to use in your code writing include:

.e55   //these are illegal because they are missing the fraction or the integer

210f: //these are illegal because they don't have the exponent or the decimal

510E   //these are illegal because they have an incomplete exponent

314159E-5L   //these are legal

3.15159   //these are legal

Boolean Literals

The next type of literal that we can discuss are the Boolean literals. There are two types that you will be able to use inside of your C++ code. Basically the Boolean values are going to be shown as either true or false. If the conditions that you set out are true, the Boolean expression is going to come out as true. On the other hand, if the conditions that you set out are not met, you are going to end up with a condition that is false. All of the answers when they are Boolean will come out either true or false.

Character Literals

When you see a character literal in your code, you will notice that they are closed off with single quotes. These can be simple and use something like 'x' to tell the command or they can be much longer in length as well. These are basic things that you are able to add into your code and can make things much easier to handle.

String Literals

Another type of literal that you are able to work with are the string literals. These are the ones that will be closed off using a double quote. The string is going to contain characters that are like the character literals, including options like universal, escape sequence, and plain characters. You can use the string literal in many ways including to break up one of your lines into two, and separating out things to make it easier to read. Some of the examples of the strings that you can use include:

hello, Mother"

"hello, \

Mother"

"hello, " "M" "other"

Learning how to use some of these different parts inside of the C++ programming language will make a big difference in how well you are able to use this computer language. Have some fun and experiment with using them a bit and you will find that it is easier than ever to get the results that you want!

Conclusion

Thank you again for purchasing this book. I hope that it proved to be informational, but enjoyable. Keep this book as a guide not only for knowledge, but inspiration as well. C++ seems like an intimidating language but the more you practice it in regularity, by days, months, and years, you will achieve complete mastery of this programming language like with anything else in life. I ask you not to fret and be anxious and a problem arise, because there will be many times in which this will happen. There are numerous resources out there for you just waiting to be read of discovered and it is in your best interest to do your due diligence in learning, improving, and enhancing your C++ programming skills to the next level.

Bonus: Brief Hacking History and Overview

Many people have heard the name C++ but really think nothing of it. If you are not very technologically versed then you may think that it is about having a mediocre letter grade, but that is not the case.

Believe it or not, C++ is a hacking language, and while it is not the only one out there, it is one of the more important ones because it is versatile and also easy to use. To learn the most about C++, you have to know more about the reason it came about and that would be hacking.

Hacking

Hacking is not a new concept. For as long as there has been any type of technologies around, there have been people figuring out ways to hack them. Hacking is the manipulations and/or interruptions of any technological stream of data that is being sent from one place to another. This is done with scripts. While you can get pre-packaged scripts online, many people prefer the old fashioned way of writing their own scripts, as is gives them more flexibility to do what the want with the information. Scripts that come already set up into packages have limited mobility and are pretty visible. The goal of a hacker who truly wants to hack is to remain discreet. If you are caught, unless you have permission to be doing what you are doing, you can get in a heap of trouble.

History of Hacking

Hacking began officially in the 1970s when teenagers were banned from using the phone lines because they were trying to make free calls, and figured out how to do so. Phone hacking was the biggest thing, and continued for over a hundred years. Making calls used to be expensive, especially when the phone lines were new, so of course people were trying to find ways to save money, and usually it caught up with them. Such was the case for a man named John Draper. He was arrested for figuring out how to make long distance calls simply by blowing a note into the receiver that prompted it to make a long distance call without an operator. You could then input the number and talk as long as you wish. Genius, but illegal.

He started a revolution though. A group of young teens banded together to create a phone line that hacked the system to help people make free calls. Once this spread like wild fire, Steve Jobs decided to come up with a product that he could market that hacked the phone lines and helped people make free calls by themselves.

Big time computer hacking didn't actually start until the 1980s. However, once it began, it spread like wildfire, and there were a lot of people who thought that it would be a great idea to see what all they could do, and how they could manipulate these computers.

Types of Hacking

There are several different types of hacking out there. And while the media portrays all hackers as bad, they are not. It is not black and white either. While those are the two most popular groups when talking about hacking, there are so many categories in between, that it would not be beneficial to only talk about the two that are most known.

The two main categories that all the sub categories fall between however, are ethical and unethical hacking.

Ethical hacking is hacking that is used only for good purposes. There are a lot of people who have full permissions to hack into a system, and to find all of the bugs of the software or hardware.

Ethical hackers are the ones that are responsible for all of the bug fixes in your phone, apps, tablets, or computers. These people are hired by a company to figure out what is wrong with their systems, and find the best way to fix it. These hackers are an essential part of the hacking community.

If it were not for hackers we would not have the world wide web, urls or HTML. Hacking is an important part if done within the boundaries of ethical hacking.

Unethical hacking, however, is not within the realms of hacking that is legal with current laws. It is hacking for a malicious purpose. People who hack bank mainframes and steal people's credit card and account information and use it to drain accounts are known as unethical hacking.

Unethical hacking is the bane of true hackers existence. These people are the ones that give the good guys a bad name.

Now to go on to the terms for all different types of hackers.

- White Hat Hackers: These are the completely ethical hackers. Every thing that they do is done for good. They go thru a system, and comb it down for any bugs, and build super strong firewalls so that the systems are safe. They create anti-malware software.

- Black Hat Hacking: This is the type of hacking that you have to stay away from. With great power comes great responsibility. The great responsibility to not become prey to the temptation that is black hat hacking. This type of hacking can get you in a lot of trouble, and are immoral. Hacking government files or even other people's privacy can be tempting but will lead to heavy disciplinary actions.

- Grey Hat Hacking: These are the hackers that sometimes do bad things for good reasons. Such as Anonymous. They may hack the firewall of an sensitive information file, but they do so to expose the corruption that is going on behind the firewall. These hackers are often treated like criminals, but in reality, they can be regarded as heroes depending on your perspective.

- Red Hats: These are the bounty hunters of the hacking world. They use their hacking skills to find illegal hackers, such as black hat hackers, or grey hats that are doing bad things that they should not be doing. They then turn them over to the feds, so that the illegal hackers are arrested. There are several other terms for these hackers, but they are not very appropriate, so we shall leave them out.

- Blue Hat Hackers: These are the blue collar workers of the hacking world. They sit in a cubicle and hack away all day to find bugs for Microsoft or other major companies. They clock into a nine to five job that just happens to involve hacking.

These are the main classifications of hackers. There are also elite hackers that spend their entire life becoming the best hackers that the world has seen, and green hat hackers who don't really care about hacking, they just do it for fun. Hacking can be a very useful tool, and even become a profession if you go about it the right way.

Now it is important to note that all of these hackers are going to work in a different way, but they are going to use the same kinds of codes in order to get the information that they want from other computers. A black hat hacker is going to concentrate on getting into the system and getting the information that they need to see success while the white hat hackers are going to work to keep these hackers off the system. While they are working in different ways, they are going to use the same tools and see who will come out on top in the end.

With that said, you need to be careful about what you are doing with your hacking abilities. If you are using them to get onto a system or a network that you aren't allowed to be on, then you could get into a lot of trouble. While some people find these vulnerabilities and tell the company all about them right away, it is still a legal issue if you are on the system when you shouldn't be. The company you mess with could press charges so it is always best to just work within your own network and keep that safe rather than trying to get onto a network you don't belong.

On the other hand, if you are someone who loves to work in the computer world and you want to be able to do this all the time, it may be a good idea to work as a white hat hacker. There are many companies that hold onto private and personal information for their customers, whether it is hospital information, credit card information, or something else. They are always on the lookout for a black hat hacker who may try to get into the system and take this information and a good white hat hacker can always find the work that they need helping these companies out.

Data Analytics: Practical Data Analysis and Statistical Guide to Transform and Evolve Any Business

Leveraging the power of Data Analytics, Data Science, and Predictive Analytics for Beginners

By Isaac D. Cody

DATA ANALYTICS

PRACTICAL DATA ANALYSIS AND STATISTICAL GUIDE TO TRANSFORM AND EVOLVE ANY BUSINESS

Leveraging the power of Data Analytics, Data Science, and Predictive Analytics for Beginners

ISAAC D. CODY

Table of Contents

Preview of this book

Have you ever wanted to use data analytics to support your business?

With many businesses, data analytics can save it. It's a great system to see how things are going, and you can collect the information to form conclusions through this. But how does it work? What are the nuances of this? Well, that's where this book comes in.

In this book, you'll learn the following:

-   What are data analytics

-   The importance of big data

-   How to conduct data analytics

-   Why a business needs this for success and prosperity now, and in the future

With data analytics, you can save your business, and this book will further prove to you the importance of this subject, what it can do for you, and how you can use data analytics to make your business shine and grow

Introduction

Hello and thank you for taking the time to check out this book!

For many of us, we want to improve our businesses, and we work to find solutions that give us the option to do that. However, there is something that every business should know about, but it's not something everyone has knowledge about.

Data analytics

Data analytics is something that can make, break, help or harm your business. If you don't educate yourself, it could end up backfiring on you, causing you to lose your treasured business. Data analytics tell you what's really going on, and what you can use these to your success. But how do you do that? How do you use this in your business to tell you about it?

Well, that's where this book comes in. By the end of this book, you'll know what you need to know about data analytics, the ins and outs of it, and how to utilize the power of data to have a successful business or any endeavors for that matter. By the end of this, you'll have data analytics at your fingertips, and you'll be able to use this successfully, and have better, more reliable and sustained results.

I used to never use data analytics, but soon, I realized just how bad of a mistake that was. It is a large one, and I started to feel the effects of it. I'm writing this book to tell you about data analytics, why they matter, and the nuances of this that can literally save your business now, and into the future.

responsibility or blame be held against the publisher for any reparation, damages, or monetary loss due to the information herein, either directly or indirectly.

Respective authors own all copyrights not held by the publisher.

The information herein is offered for informational purposes solely, and is universal as so. The presentation of the information is without contract or any type of guarantee assurance.

The trademarks that are used are without any consent, and the publication of the trademark is without permission or backing by the trademark owner. All trademarks and brands within this book are for clarifying purposes only and are the owned by the owners themselves, not affiliated with this document.

Chapter 1: What Are Data Analytics and Why Every Business Should Have It

Data analytics is very important, but you might wonder what it is, and what is so special about it. Well, this chapter will go over what it is, why it matters, and why it is essential for every and any business.

Data Analytics

Data analytics is a simple idea at the core of it all. It is looking at raw data to draw a conclusion about the information. That means, you'll have a set of data here, and it's used to help show the company what's really going on in order to make better decisions and it allows you to see if an existing business model or theory is working. Data analytics is done to look and analyze what is going on. We'll go over the anatomy of how you get there with this later on, but in essence, it is basically the use of software and trends to identify patterns and to look for hidden relationships.

For example, let's say that you're looking at the amount of items you've sold within the year. Let's say it was going great at first, but around June or July, things start to fizzle out. At first, you might freak out, but upon further analysis, you might realize that you put in a new program, or maybe hired on a new person to the business. Maybe Joe Schmo might be causing you more harm than good, and when you look at his production, you'll start to see who is at fault here in order to handle it accordingly.

In another sort of situation, maybe sales started to increase. The wrong thing to do is to think this is some act of god or something of that nature. Rather, look at it from an analytics standpoint. Perhaps, you cut the costs on a product or got rid of one product and kept another. These choices matter, and the purpose of this is to draw a conclusion based upon the data at hand.

Data analytics isn't something new, as this has been around since the 1950s on a larger scale in some ways. Many people use basic analytics to help them look for various insights and trends, but there are other larger ways to see where things might go.

This is <u>key</u> to know where to look and see where things are heading. Forecasting is one of the most essential elements to data analytics. We will go over this in more detail later in the book.

With data analytics, you can have it at a holistic level, where you can get the information, run it through the software, and then get the information, and from there, the owner or the person running the business can make an immediate decision. It's important to have this, and it doesn't take much to learn it.

Why Businesses need this

It should be fairly obvious as to why a business would need this, but maybe explaining it this way may shed some new light on this topic.

For starters, think about every single decision you've made in a business. Most of the time, the sound, rational decisions in a business were backed by evidence, whether that evidence may be graphs or the like. Business analytics allows you to do this. You can look at the online analytical processing or other sorts of data and see where things are going. This will allow you to make decisions.

If you're running a consulting firm, and maybe you're monitoring how many clients each consultant takes on, you can see which employees aren't fitting the bill, and who is doing above and beyond. This in turn will keep toxic and bad people from getting into the company, protecting yourself and the others around you.

In the same vein, maybe you have a person who is going above and beyond, who should be promoted and given a raise because they're working hard. You can use this as a basis to promote people, on the grounds of the statistical evidence. You can do this in order to keep morale going. Sometimes, if you don't reward the ones doing well, you'll end up suffering because the person will then not work as well, causing issues for you too.

But also, look at it in other regards as well. It can even protect you from bad situations. For example, let's say that you're running a bank or a credit card service. These companies and businesses will look at any withdrawal and spending of a certain person at any time. If they suddenly see countless amount of money withdrawn from there, it actually can be grounds for fraud. This is why cards will get cancelled, because they notice the problem and take action. Think about it, you wouldn't want to wake up with a severely negative balance, would you? This is used for your own protection, and these businesses know that.

Furthermore, perhaps you have an employee that seems fine, but upon data analysis, you see that they have been embezzling from you for a bit now. You can stop this situation from happening to the point where you catch them before they blow off the company and you're left with nothing.

Now, a business also needs this not just for protection, but for their products as well. Let's say you have an online business that sells different types of clothing. Maybe you have the data on all of the articles of clothing and you see that some are being sold more than other products. These data analyses will allow you to see which products your customers will buy more or less, and you can adjust this accordingly so that you're not wasting money. In this day and age, many of these analytics have dashboards that showcase these data streams so that you can see them in real time.

When you get right down to it, it's downright essential to have data analytics. After all, have you ever tried running a business with no information on what's good and bad, no idea on what will and won't sell? You don't. You sit there wondering why in the world you don't have customers, why your business is failing and why you're not doing the best. Plus, it can be used in the other way as well. It can tell you just what you need. A business needs this, because it will showcase to them what they need to fix before it's too late. This can utterly save you, and while you might not have liked doing this back in high school during math class, it's one of the most important things you can do for your company.

So, at the bottom of all of this is the essential notion that you data analytics. It's imperative to the survival of your business. If you refuse to put in the effort of analyzing your business, then you're simply losing out. In the other hand, properly disseminating data can truly not only make your business successful, but also make you stand out from the rest of your competition.

Chapter 2: How to Handle Large Amounts of Data and the Benefits of It

With data analytics, you'll be looking at the various amounts of data, and it seems terrifying at first. You might wonder what you should do in this case, and how to handle it. Well, this chapter will go over how you can handle these large amounts of data, and how you can use this to benefit from it.

Handling the Data

With small businesses, it might not be as bad, but with large businesses, you might start to wonder how you're going to handle something so immense. Well, you got a few options, and these are essential to your understanding of data analytics, and in turn it can save your bacon in terms of understanding and using this for your own personal success.

- **Online analytical processing**: this is referred to as OLAP, and this is a computer processing software that allows the user to get data from different points of view. For example, you can have the data analyzed on a spreadsheet in one case to look at the revenue of one product in comparison to another.

OLAP software is a multidimensional database, and this will consider every single data attributed as something else. You can look at this from a grand level, such all of the products that you have sold in specific regions in order to display them. These can be used on a much broader scale in order to find out various facets of it.

- **Real-time analytics**: This is essentially taking all of the available data at the time and looking at it immediately. For example, this will give you all of the sales for the day based on the data entered into the system. It will also be based by the hour and by the minute depending on what interval is most needed to you. This is definitely great if you want to know how things are doing in real time and this is essential for any sort of data that is volatile in their nature. If you're doing anything with investment, real-time analytics is important to have in order to be successful with this. A good example of this being used is in customer relations management that can tell you about of the customers are and the interaction and how they're actually feeling about the services rendered to them in order to precut whether or not you can fix the issue with certain people, or if there is anything to fix at all.

- **Dynamic analysis**: Dynamic analysis is an offline version of looking through the data as it changes over time. This is used to debug programs and allows you to create situations in order to produce either errors or corrections. This type of analysis allows you to forecast specific needs of your business. By doing this, you can presumably reduce the cost of the testing and the maintenance of something. It can also look for the unnecessary parts of your business, and makes sure that it's tested properly in a given amount of time. Because it is offline, you would need prior data to use this type of analysis. However, you can run this simultaneously with real time, and essentially dynamic analysis takes the data that is there, changes it so that it can be used for future usage.

- **Statistical analysis**: This type of analysis involves collecting and disseminating every data from every sample set. Simple statistical analyses consist of graphs, charts, and anything that has visual aspects of statistics. It also includes the measures of average, location, skews, variance, and standard deviations. These are essential in analyzing in sort of information and are one that most adults are aware of. Many statistical packages will include type of analysis already. Excel is one of the most used and basic software for statistical analyses. However, it does lack advance statistical analyses like multivariates, statistical errors, in depth hypothesis testing, associations, test statistics, and other correlational evidence. Though these are more complex and advanced type of statistics, a good software to have in analyzing your business is SPSS.

- **Predictive analysis**: After all the data has been collected, it's simply used to predict something in the future. This in turn will allow you to see what needs to be fixed, and from there, you can determine the idea of where things will go at this point. This branch of analytics includes data mining, modeling, machine learning, and artificial intelligence to analyze and scrutinize current data to make predictions about the future. Chapter 4 touches upon this subject.

The Process of Handling
When handling large amounts of data, you'll easily get overwhelmed. It's obvious how this is, and in general, it's best if you get software for this to asset you. That'll be discussed in

detail later, but this section will go over how to handle this when it hits you.

First, is to be calm. The sheer amount of this is enough to make anyone go mad. But you shouldn't get frustrated. Instead, you should take everything that you're reading, analyze it, determine what to do with it next, and then go from there. Don't overwhelm yourself, because it'll just hurt you later on. Take everything with a grain of salt and ask yourself, "how will all this data benefit me?"

Take the statistics of those that are the most important first. We'll go over the data that is most important and see where that leads to. You should look this over, see how things are changing with the company, and then go from there.

Make sure to visualize this data. Get graphs and charts out so you can see this. Numbers do communicate some aspects of this, but don't let that be the defining point of it all. Instead, let that be a part of this, and from there, you can go over what you should do as a result of this newfound information.

If you see that there is something going on, don't despair, but instead, take what you see, get it written down, and handle that. Remember, these statistics do change. You're the one who changes them. It won't magically happen by looking at it, you've got to do something about it. Even if it means firing a bad employee or getting rid of a product that you've been selling, it does make all the difference.

Make sure to pay attention to these numbers and look to compare, not just recently, but far back. A common problem with those who handle large amounts of data, is they will only look at the temporary instead of the long term. If you do that however, you will not get to the level, or beyond the level that you are in right now. Extrapolate data from days ago, weeks ago, but more importantly, extrapolate data from *years* ago. Many businesses do not see how important it is to do this. You'll be stuck in that range if you look at data from a short time period, so make sure that you have the whole picture painted for you before you make a decision.

When you're analyzing this, get someone else to help you, such as an assistant or someone who knows how to read the charts. You'll thank yourself later, because for one, this can be overwhelming. Plus, sometimes having the second person there can be essential. It can tell you whether or not the decision that you're about to make is the best thing to do, and if you should go through with the actions at hand. It could save your business if you look at it in that way, and you'll feel better about it too. Plus, sometimes having someone else there will help fester new ideas, so if you want to take a different approach to a problem in your business, hiring someone else like a statistician or a data analyst is definitely worth investing.

Benefits of Handling data analytics yourself

It is apparent that there are many benefits to handling these large amounts of data, but did you know the extent of this? This chapter will go over the bigger picture, the reason as to why you need to become comfortable with the parts of collecting the data you need and looking at it to form a conclusion, for it can save your business.

- It'll accelerate the time that it takes and you will make faster decision-making. What many people don't realize is that many times, decision-making falls upon making some decisions not based on facts. That's wrong, and instead, you need to do this based off the information that you have at hand. It'll allow for better, more smarter decisions that will impact the business. Of course, the biggest problems many analyst go thru is using the data at hand or using your gut feeling. Inevitably you're going to have to make decision based on your instincts but at the same time, a savvy business man or woman will make those gut decision after the data has been analyzed.

- It'll optimize the business to best suit your needs. You might not be running at the peak efficiency of the business, and sometimes, even the smallest changes will make a difference. Make sure that your business is optimized for success so that you're not sitting there scratching your head as you wonder why your business revenue is down and why production is lacking. Remember, you're the one who makes the difference in the big picture.

- Increasing personal efficiency is another major benefit. Let's face it, we can all get more efficient in life. We could all do better, but what if we managed to make ourselves better? By tackling this and looking at the big picture, you can make a difference, and it does show itself with time. Make sure that you're working towards success and efficiency as well, and don't sit around dawdling on the small stuff instead of doing something good for yourself. One of the best advice for any business owner is assign someone to do the minuscule task of small data management and allow yourself to make those *big* decisions.

- Getting new revenue and driving in various new revenue sources can be a major benefit to this. Sometimes with data analytics, we might end up discovering a whole new line of income we didn't know about before, and it does make a difference. Some people might have missed that one revenue source of place that they weren't viewing before, and they could end up screwing themselves over because of this.

- You can also improve the competitiveness over other business rivals. Some businesses do use this, but some do not, and that is a fatal mistake. Some people won't catch their issues or see the benefits until it's too late. They go around thinking that everything is fine, when in essence, they're in denial. *Always* tackle problems head on. It's easy to let problems slide but a good businessperson will not let any stone unturned. Analyze everything and find out the problem. Once you solve, you'll thank yourself later in the future for that one small problem may have turned into something that is unmanageable in the future.

- It helps as well to showcase business problems. Sometimes some of these problems might be eating away at the business, but if you look at this, seeing the large amounts of data that are going on, you'll see the difference it does make, and you'll be able to see that the business problems that will be addressed because of this. It can really help showcase major issues and allow you to see just what in the world is going on as well.

Chapter 3: Types of Data Analytics

With data analytics, it's important to understand that some types of data analytics are not the same as others. Remember, that this big data can help with fraud detection as said before, the competitive analysis on a complex level, optimizing various structures such as call centers, seeing customers feel on a real-time level, improving the traffic management of various intelligence, and also to even help manage other such items. All of these things can be used with data analytics, and big data is definitely something that you need in order to help you fully understand your business.

But did you know that there are types of data analytics underneath all of this. There are various factors that are part of both, and it's important to realize just what they are, the versions of this, and examples of their use. You don't want to let things go by the wayside when trying to understand something. This chapter will go over the four major types of big data analytics, and also some of the factors of what they entail, along with examples on how these fit into the real world, and how they're used.

Three Factors

Now all big data analytics does have three various parts to these, and these are what make up big data and data analytics.

The first is **volume**. You will see with big data that it's hard to handle all of this at once. That's why you're given various different types of data analytics, and you'll be able to use these for various potions. With smaller businesses sometimes this concept of volume does come in, but as your business tends to grow and shape itself, you'll see that this element of volume does play a part. Too little volume doesn't show much of a change, but too much can really be a problem for you. That's why with big data analytics, and data analytics in general, you must take into account the volume of things.

Then there is the **velocity**. This is how fast the data is flowing in and out. Now some places might have data analytics that are easy to see, since the data is moving at a speed comfortable for a human's pace. But, in certain other cases, like in the case with a call center or an electric company's power grid, you'll notice that the data moves unbearably fast. Big-time companies need to watch this section of data analytics like a hawk, because while you can certainly sift through the big stuff, but becomes problematic over time if you don't manage the speed of this, and that's why it's a major factor in the way the business is conducted at the core.

Then there is the **variety**. The variety is the difference in handling the big data. With smaller companies, it's all pretty cut and narrow, with very little difference but as you start to grow, you will start to develop departments, and various other functions. These departments and the like will have functions under that which need to be measured. For example take a look at AT&T and the traffic they possess, and see if there is a way for them to handle all of that without big data analytics? There isn't, and that's why it's important to realize that you do need this in order to help you make sure that you get the most results from this. So you need big data analytics to see just from the sheer variety of them all, and you'll see why this is important and ties into the other two when we go over the four types.

Four Types of Data Analytics

From what you saw earlier, big data basically is what you use to manage the organization effectively. You need to make sure that the analytics are put in as well, and you need these analytics to have a place in the company, because if you don't, you won't be able to see the hidden patterns or anything that is wrong along with the relationships of various elements. But with this, you need to know of the various types as well, and that's what will come next.

- **Descriptive**: Descriptive analytics was described earlier in the chapter. Essentially, this is the type of data analytics that is said to be based upon what's happening now with the data that is coming in. Typically, to look for this type of analytics, you will use a dashboard that displays all of this data. Location of averages, ranges, standard deviation are some of the basic descriptive statistics and analytics that are covered in this topic.

- **Diagnostic**: This is the type of data analytics that will look to past performance and will tell you what was going on, why that was, and the result of it. The question this type of analytic asks is, "Why did it happen?"

- **Prescriptive**: Prescriptive analytics will tell you when it's time to take action. Now, this is the most important one of them all, because this is the data analytics that will tell you what needs to be done next, and it's sort of what will determine the next step of the company. This is the type of data analytics that either lets the company go under, or will let the company spring forward as a result.

- **Predictive**: this is more of a prediction of what's going on in order to determine the future course of action and the scenarios that might happen as a result of this. This is a sort of predictive forecast is important because it tells you what to do and where to go before you begin with changing or starting things up in your business.

Examples of These Analytics

A big part of understanding data analytics is not just reading about I, but seeing examples of it. This chapter will discuss each of the various types of data analytics, and how they're used in big businesses.

Prescriptive analytics, as said before, are the most valuable, but it's not the most used. For example, only 13% of the organizations reporting on this type of data analytics use predictive, but only 3% are using prescriptive.

For example, many people like to use this to predict what's going on, but the prescription of the correct action can make a difference. When you have big data analytics that talks about a certain subject, these prescriptive analytics will give you a focus on the various questions. Let's take for example the health care industry, and you're working on the hospital's analytics based on the sick people that are coming in. Maybe you want to manage the amount of obese person cases to see how you can work on focusing the treatment. You can look at the various types, such as bad cholesterol, diabetes, or other disorders, and you should use this to focus on the type of treatments they should take. Maybe you want to go over the problems with inner-city youth as well. You can use prescriptive analytics to give you a bright picture on what is going on.

Predictive analytics are used for the past patterns that have come up with the purpose to predict the future. For example, you can use predictive analytics to use for sales lead scores. Some companies can use this to see where the best sorts of sales leads come from, and you can use this for the entire sales process, such as the amount and types of communications, the presence of social media, and other such factors. Predictive analytics is helpful to bolster up the sales and to support them so that they get better, improve the marketing that is going on, and improve sales forecasts as well.

Diagnostic analytics is used to see why something happened. This is important especially when you start to have big changes.

For example, let's say that you have a social media campaign going on within Facebook. You might start to see a spring up in numbers, and you might wonder why. Well, if you use diagnostic analysis, you can see the posts, followers, various mentions, the types of fans, how many people viewed the page, any sorts of reviews, any sorts of favoring, and other such things. You might start to see a whole lot of various mentions, but sometimes that one sort of mention might be what caused the whole situation to progress, and that's why as a social media manager, it can be improve to have this going on.

Finally there is descriptive analytics, and this is basically the lowest one on the data value chain. This is basically getting the information in order to look for various patterns in order to give insight to this sort of thing. For example, you can look at a person's credit history to see the credit risk of them before you allow them to get money out of you. Maybe you look through the background of a person before hiring, in order to see what they were like beforehand. These are important, and if you have this, you can sometimes use it to build onto the other three types of analytics.

Understanding big data analytics adds a ton of value towards your business. In a sense, it does tell a story, because it will reduce a lot of complexities to actual actionable items in order to help you make better business decisions. If you know how to use this, then you can increase your business by tenfold.

Chapter 4: Big Data, Data Mining, Data Warehousing, and Data Visualization

Now that you know a bit about what data analytics are and the nuances of them, it's time to go over the other parts of this, such as how it's used, and other such factors. This chapter will go over a few concepts, and it'll help you understand how this is used in a company.

Big Data

The first thing to go over is big data. Big data, as sad before, is data that doesn't have a small amount. It spans over a ton of various areas, and that's what data analytics does with it. With big data, you're looking at a much bigger picture than you expect it to be.

Big data can sometimes be big in the sheer volume of it all. If you take for example a call center, you will see how big that data is. The call center is a large sort of structure, with many people working within it, and because of how big it is, there needs to be a way to look over the data.

Big data helps larger companies make the correct decisions when it comes to future endeavors. It's sort of a security against wrongly-made decisions, and sometimes, when you have a large amount, you're able to pinpoint the patterns of things, seeing how various smaller patterns affect the larger ones at time. You'll be able to see the various transactions and everything that goes along with it in order to form a rightful conclusion as a result.

Big data is really what you use to collect it, and you need to use data mining in order to find everything that you need to find.

Data mining

Now, since you have all of this data there for you, sometimes you need to find what you're looking for. Remember, not all data is made equally, especially in the realm of looking at big data. You don't necessarily need the data from everything right there in front of you, but you need some sort of semblance of understanding of it, and you need realistic data to discuss what to do next.

This is where data mining comes in. in essence, data mining is looking at various types of data from different sort of sources and perspectives and then putting into summary the information that is seemed useful to the business. In essence, this is the data that will increase the revenue of the business, reduce the costs that you have, or even sometimes both. Often, data mining is done with software and other analytical tools that can be used to find the data. This will allow users to look at data from different types of angles, put it into categories, and then put in summary the relationships that you see. In essence, data mining is looking for correlations and patterns in their larger databases.

So, you have all of this information here, correct? You will see that this technology is much more powerful, and with the aid of computers, it's able to soft through many different scanners and such, and you can look at the processing of order in order to see what is working to increase the revenue of the business, and what is working to hurt the business as a result.

With data mining, you'll be able to get the data from various resources, allow yourself to look at various internal factors that you might o tee at the onset, and you'll be able to change things or leave them the same, which in turn can have a significant impact on the sales of such items, the satisfaction of a customer, and even profits in a sense. At the end of it, you're pretty much putting everything there into summary and various transactional segments in order to make sure that you have the right ideas. For example, various video rent services can change up the database in order to get more rentals that will increase the amount of customers renting. In a sense, this takes the big data as talked about before, sifts through it, and with the powerful software, you get a full and cohesive idea on what exactly you're going for, and the results of it as well. Remember, that data mining is definitely the link between the transactions and the systems, and it will look for those relationships based on the transactions in order for form an analytical conclusion thus from these relationships.

Data warehouse

Now, once you have all of that data, you need to figure out where it's supposed to go, right? Well, there is an option for you to find this, and in essence, it's a software known as the data warehouse. This is a system that is used when you have a data analysis, and in a sense, it's where all of the information is stored when going through various data analysis. This is another major component of business intelligence, and for a good reason.

A data warehouse is a group of repositories that are putting data into different areas from sources that aren't always the same. This takes for example various historical data and even some data on recent events in order to create a good, analytical report for those what are working in the business. For example, it will take the quarterly comparisons that a business might have, and then put the trends up next to the detailed sales analysis done daily. From there, you can take the information from the data warehouse, and the current information you've gotten from mining, and you'll be able to use this in order to form connections.

Now, the data warehouse is essentially uploaded onto the computer from the various operational systems. The marketing, sales, and the rest of the important facets of the business will soon be integrated into there. The data will then go towards a sort of operational data store in order to go to the data warehouse in order to report it later on.

Now, what this will do is that it'll take the data from various sources into one database in order to present data, and along with that it'll help with the problem of database isolation contention with the transitions. This will be able to allow the transactions to still happen despite it all.

Also, look at it in a sort of data history sense. If you really need to go back, you can look at it. This will also help because sometimes the transactions systems might not have the data that you need, and you might have to do some digging. It saves the time and you'll be able to look for this easily, and without fail.

It also works to help improve the data quality. Often, when you're going through a lot of data, there are some bad data that comes about, and sometimes the codes and descriptions are off. However, with a data warehouse, you'll be able to have all of that consistently put into there, and there is anything wrong with it, you'll be able to fix some of the bad data and even take it down. From there, you can then present this in a more consistent manner, and then change up the structure in order to make it easier to the various users of the business. A data warehouse, from there, will allow you to make various decisions and queries about various facets of this much easier, and over time, you'll be able to take the receptacle of this useful information, put it all out there nicely, and from there, form a good, cohesive decision one very thing that you will do with it.

Data warehousing is very important with a big data situation, because it'll allow you to make it easier on yourself, make it easier on others, and you'll be able to take all of this and have a good idea of where it all fits much easier.

Data Visualization

Now, this is sort of the final picture and part of all of this. This is data visualization. In essence, when you're dealing with big data, the sheer amount and velocity of it, not to mention the fact that it can be all over the place, can make you feel like you're going mad. Well, if you feel confusion when looking at all of those numbers, wouldn't it make sense to visualize them? The best thing to do is to use data visualization, which is the display graphically of various abstract information for two different reasons. It's used to help you make sense of various patterns and other elements for one, which is called data analysis, and the other reason is communication to others. If you want to get something done and fixed up, you've got to communicate this effectively, and that's where data visualization comes in. Many companies will live off of this data, and for many people, the data visualization will allow you to understand what is going on, along with understanding how to present them to other people. The information is abstract, because it is statistics and not physical things. Sure, statistics might represent physical products or information, but it's really a statistic and some numbers at the bottom of it all. These visualizations really work for anything, such as sales, performance, or the like, and when it doesn't pertain to the physical world, these can still be used, because it'll give form to something that doesn't have any form. Many of these will translate form abstract to visual through the visuals given to yourself. You can look at the designs of these as well.

Typically, these are measured in graphs more than anything. As said, a picture is worth over 1000 words, and that is the case with this. You can look at this, and you will start to see the way things change.

Now, you could look at these numbers without it. I don't recommend it very well, but sometimes, you just need to look at an actual representation in order to fully comprehend that. Big data uses these visuals, and often they are a graph with some statistics point, and from there, you'll be able to see the various values that are contained within this, and from there, you'll see the trends necessary within this, which will allow you to be more successful with this.

In essence, the visualization is the final step in this before making the decisions. It's what will showcase the data in order to improve the conditions, and it's what you need in order to be successful.

Now, data mining and the other parts of big data are used altogether in order to effectively create the picture that you're looking for. This chapter allowed you to see the ways these all worked together, and how they can continue to work together in order to form great and understanding sorts of situations for you to use with data analysis as well.

Chapter 5: How to Conduct Data Analysis on Your Own Business

Now that you know of data analysis and what it's all about, it's time to go over how to do it yourself on your own business. Now, you probably won't need to use a big software to do this. After all, we're not going after big data as of yet, but this chapter will go over how to do it in order to be successful in a step-by-step fashion

1) Get an electronic database and organize your data. The best resource to use this for is Microsoft Excel. This will allow you to work in a new file that you can edit. You should copy the data into there. Don't do this in the master file because this could cause possible corruption while analyzing. You can then organize all of the data into there, along with using filters to make it easier for you to see the difference. You should make sure that you take your time with this, because the last thing you want to do is to put it in the wrong places.

2) Now, you will then need to code your text responses with numbers. What this means is that for some answers,

you will need to code these into various numbers before you analyze it. You can develop your own coding for this, based on the formation that you get with the data. For example, let's say you're analyzing sales data. You have three products. Assign number one to the first product, two to the second, and three to the third.

3) Once that's done, start to create a good system to group it all. If you're working with actual human responses, which you might be, or maybe just products, you might want to protect the confidentiality by putting some numbers or letter by this. You should try to keep all of the groups on separate various sheets within the document, or in different columns and rows if you're using the same sheet. You should make sure that the people or items are rightfully grouped together before you analyze.

4) At this point, check it all for mistakes. Sometimes, when you're putting data in and copying various items, you might not check the master file. You should do this periodically, because it's not unheard of that some people mix up numbers or put them in the wrong place, and if that happens, your data becomes useless. Don't do that, and instead check it before you move on.

5)   Now, you can compare the various tests by doing a t-test. These are typically used to compare the averages of these samples. You have a sample test to determine what to do in order to see where it falls in the value. You can use a two-sample t-test in order to test that the groups are different. For example, you can use the one-sample in product manufacturing in order to see the values so you can see the difference, but if you're doing a clinical study, try out a two-sample t-test.

6)   You can now use ANOVA in order to look at the various results of the groups in order to compare the means of these groups. It's typically used in biomedical, but it's good for any sort of group. If you're using a one-way ANOVA, you might use that to compare the means of many groups to the control group. You can use the two-way ANOVA in order to compare the different means between various groups. This can be used if you have a various product with different variables, or maybe you're looking at the performance and hours of various workers in comparison to the results of the company for that week.

7)   You can now use linear regression in order to see the variation in the dependent variable, which is what

basically another relies on. The test is used to check out the strength between both of these variables, much as maybe if you were looking at the speed of a sale to the speed of getting a product out, and in that case you would choose to use linear regression for this.

8)   From this point, you use ANCOVA in order to compare the relationships of the two various groups to the same variable that you have out. This will allow you to control the difference of the variation between the independent variable and both of the groups. You can check to see if the two groups of products had the same sales rates at the different times with this. You'll have to use two different linear regression lines to look at it, so make sure that you keep that before you continue on.

9)   Now, you can check out other sorts of data collecting sight, such as OHLP and other sorts of statistical collecting sites that can assist you. There are a lot of tests out there, and while there are some common ones, there are variations of these tests that might be best for your data. You should look online or for other sorts of software to help with this.

10)   Next, you define the research questions. You should never lose

focus of the study that you're doing or the analysis, and you should make sure that you stick to the research that you're given and the variables of this. You should make sure that you collect the right data that will answer your questions, and you will start to see the answers as you work with this.

11) At this point as well, it might be best to get that other person in. Now, with big data statistics, these get very complicated, very fast, especially if the data sets are huge and unchanging. With a dashboard of these, you'll be getting them in real time, and make sure that you do talk with someone who knows of the stats and have a consolation before you continue so that you can make sure that you make the correct decision of this. You should look to see if you need to change things, if one area was overlooked, or the like, because you don't want to make the incorrect decision which could cost it all for you.

12) Now, from here, you can then implement the action. Chose the action that you've done based off of the analysis, whether it be taking out a product, implementing a new sales campaign, or firing someone. From there, you should then run the test to see how things go.

13) Now, you can then come back to this, put in the new data into the data warehouse, take the past data, compare it, and from there, make further decisions. Sometimes, you can even work on more data and graphs in order to have a better visual representation of things and to have quality figures for this. You should make sure that you have all of these there before you make the final call so you do make the best decision possible.

14) You should make sure that if you come across data that is similar, that you group it together. If you don't, you might end up overlooking it, so do take the time to get this started out.

15) From here, you can call on other software and tests as necessary, but it's not necessarily the case. Just continue to watch the patterns and trends, make models of the regression of these various points, and from there, continue to make a decision on what to do with the data at hand.

With various big data and the analysis of tit, it can be quite hard to get a grip on it. However, this chapter showed you a bit more on how you go about utilizing big data in order to be efficient with it, and how to use it for your own personal success and well-being.

Chapter 6: How to use Social Media, Software, and other Tools to Sustain Your Business

Now that you know a bit about big data and how to conduct a data analysis, it's time to talk about other forms of help you have. There is software, and there is also the form of social media and other tools. This chapter will go over what they are, how they can help, and when to use them.

Software for Success

If you're looking to get into major detail on the type of data you're looking at, consider checking out software. There are a lot of software options at the forefront, and it's imperative to make sure that you do look at these options as well. This section will go over but a few of the software options that you can check out for big data collection.

- NCA calculator and Software: this is a free calculator and package in order to help you to calculate necessary conditions that are present within datasets, although they might not be sufficient. The software is an R package that is used for this. Both of these are great to help you with conditions that might be present, but haven't been discussed.

- Data applied: this is an online data mining and isolation type of software. This is good for when you don't feel like doing the calculations yourself, so you let this software mine if for you, and from there, it'll display the visuals.

- DataMelt: this is a java-based framework with a community of developers that will give a multiplatform sort of data analysis of the information that is given.

- ELKI: this is another data mining sort of framework that is also Java supported that contains data-mining visuals and the functions that go with this.

- KNIME: this is the Konstanz Information Miner. This is a user-friendly sort of comprehensive data-analysis framework that will allow you to perform data analytics in order to find various issues.

- MEPX: this is a tool that is cross-platform that will allow you to use it for regression and various class problems

- Orange: this is a visual programming sort of tool that gives you interactive data visual ions so you can look at the information provided there along with ways to analyze statistical data, various data mining, and various learning of machines.

- QSoas: this is a command-driven program that is used for analyzing various data in order to remove the noise, correct the baseline, fit the data within global solutions, and to use the differential equations of various schemes involving kinetics, and more of this. There are binaries available for this as well that work for Mac and Windows if you so want this.

- R: this is a program that is a language software as well that is used to compute various statistics in computing, along with various graphical tools.

- ROOT: this is a C++ data analysis framework that was developed by CERN

- Dotplot: this is a visual designer that is cloud based and works on the cloud drive in order to create analytic and visual models of the data presented to this sort of thing.

- DevInfo: this is a database that was supported by the UNDG that is used to look at and check out human development. This is a great sort of data analytics software and tool that can be used in order to help those look over the various facets of human development

All of these software and tools that you see here can be put into the computer in order to help with analyzing data. By using this, you'll facilitate the ability to look for plausible solutions to various problems, and from thee, you'll be able to formulate the solutions that are necessary in order to help generate better results from the statistical analysis that is coming about.

Now, with software, you have to make sure that it's strong enough to put on the computer. You should make sure that your computer has the power to run this sort of thing, and if not, you get a computer that can. Through data analytics and the tools mentioned here, it could help you figure out what you need. This software is all free, so you don't have to pay for it, and from there you'll be able to determine what sort of results you get from this type of analysis.

With tools, really the tools were listed in here, but if you have any Moe sort of data calculation tools that you discover, those are always good. Tools really just help in the overall data coverage, and in general they're a good source to have if you're looking to father understand the various nuances of a company or a set of statistics that you see and want to learn more about.

Social Media

Social media is another major part of building a business these days, not just because of the fact that everything is all out there, but also because of the analytics that go along with this. Social media is used these days in order to perform data analytics, and there are a few reasons why.

For starters, you have all of the information on every single thing that you post on social media right there. Now, the products and such might be fine, but if you're really looking to see the progress of your company, you check out the analytics.

With data analytics, you will be able to look at the traffic and performance from your page over the last month or so. You can look in general at the performance that you are presenting, and you can see whether or not things have gotten better or worse. You can see just how many people you are reaching with the page that you have, along with how many have clicked on various ads and such, and how many have agreed to follow you. These statistics might not mean much, but they can.

For example, if you get a specific sort of mention from someone, and let's say that the mention alone got you say, twenty followers, you will realize from this that the correct course of action is to keep working with that person. Perhaps you took on a new person that is representing your company in showcasing of products, or a new model for your clothing brand. If you do that, and let's say that thing start to jump all of a sudden, you'll be able to look at the data, see where it came from, any other sorts of variables and factors, and from there, continue on with the successful actions. In essence, this will allow you to continue on with those successful actions that are obviously creating something good for yourself, and for other people as well.

With social media, it'll give you the chance to really do an in-depth analysis, and in many case, you can even go back, I knew with Facebook in particular, you'll be able to go back at least a few months, up to year, to see how the page has progressed, and how things have gotten better. At the end of it all, it can certainly be something that can help you out, and by then, you'll be able to really have a much better experience with this.

With social media and all of these other tools, looking at your business and actually changing it using analytics has never been easier. For some people, it might be rocky at first but once you start to do the full analysis, looking over just what you're getting out of this, and doing something about it, you'll be able to have way more success with this, now and into the future as well as other sorts of social media endeavors too.

Conclusion

Thank you again for downloading this book!

I hope this book was able to help you to see the power of data analytics and see just what you can get out of this. Data analytics is pretty mind-blowing at the end of it all, and you'll learn quite a bit about it from this book. This book is the beginning of it all, where you'll be able to start on your adventure with data analytics. It's important to know this, because often, it can lead to many different factors, one of them being the very future and success of your business. So yes, data analytics is very important for that, and if you're a business owner looking to fortify your business and the success that you know will hold true, this is what you need to have.

The next step is to work on getting your data analytics together. First, you need to start collecting the data that you have, mining it from all of the various facets of the company. Work on keeping it together, and form there, you can create the visuals that are necessary for you to showcase the data that you have. You will soon notice the trends, what's been going on, what's been wrong, and even how to fix them. Sometimes the most shocking things can be learning the truth about your company and the fact that it's not doing well. Even so though, data analytics will help you blow right on past that, and you'll be able to be much more successful as a result of everything that you've learned from this, and the results that you've obtained.

Finally, if you enjoyed this book, then I'd like to ask you for a favor, would you be kind enough to leave a review for this book on Amazon? It'd be greatly appreciated!

Thank you and good luck!

Related Titles

[Hacking University: Freshman Edition Essential Beginner's Guide on How to Become an Amateur Hacker](#)

Hacking University: Sophomore Edition. Essential Guide to Take Your Hacking Skills to the Next Level. Hacking Mobile Devices, Tablets, Game Consoles, and Apps

Hacking University: Junior Edition.
Learn Python Computer Programming
From Scratch. Become a Python Zero to
Hero. The Ultimate Beginners Guide in
Mastering the Python Language

Hacking University: Senior Edition Linux. Optimal Beginner's Guide To Precisely Learn And Conquer The Linux Operating System. A Complete Step By Step Guide In How Linux Command Line Works

Hacking University: Graduation Edition. 4 Manuscripts (Computer, Mobile, Python, & Linux). Hacking Computers, Mobile Devices, Apps, Game Consoles and Learn Python & Linux

Data Analytics: Practical Data Analysis and Statistical Guide to Transform and Evolve Any Business, Leveraging the power of Data Analytics, Data Science, and Predictive Analytics for Beginners

C++: Learn C++ Like a Boss. A Beginners Guide in Coding Programming And Dominating C++. Novice to Expert Guide To Learn and Master C++ Fast

About the Author

Isaac D. Cody is a proud, savvy, and ethical hacker from New York City. Currently, Isaac now works for a mid-size Informational Technology Firm in the heart of NYC. He aspires to work for the United States government as a security hacker, but also loves teaching others about the future of technology. Isaac firmly believes that the future will heavily rely computer "geeks" for both security and the successes of companies and future jobs alike. In his spare time, he loves to analyze and scrutinize everything about the game of basketball.